EMMANUEL JOSEPH

The Blueprint of Standing Ovations, Crafting Speeches That Leave Audiences Breathless

Copyright © 2025 by Emmanuel Joseph

All rights reserved. No part of this publication may be reproduced, stored or transmitted in any form or by any means, electronic, mechanical, photocopying, recording, scanning, or otherwise without written permission from the publisher. It is illegal to copy this book, post it to a website, or distribute it by any other means without permission.

First edition

This book was professionally typeset on Reedsy.
Find out more at reedsy.com

Contents

1	Chapter 1: The Art of Capturing Attention	1
2	Chapter 2: Structuring for Impact	3
3	Chapter 3: The Power of Words	5
4	Chapter 4: Mastering Delivery	7
5	Chapter 5: Engaging Your Audience	9
6	Chapter 6: Crafting a Memorable Conclusion	11
7	Chapter 7: The Role of Emotion	13
8	Chapter 8: Overcoming Fear and Anxiety	15
9	Chapter 9: The Impact of Visual Aids	17
10	Chapter 10: Connecting with Diverse Audiences	19
11	Chapter 11: Handling Q&A Sessions	21
12	Chapter 12: The Journey of Continuous Improvement	23
13	Chapter 13: Utilizing Voice Modulation	25
14	Chapter 14: The Psychology of Persuasion	27
15	Chapter 15: The Role of Technology in Modern Public Speaking	29

1

Chapter 1: The Art of Capturing Attention

In the realm of public speaking, the opening lines of your speech are pivotal. This chapter dives into the essence of making a lasting first impression. An attention-grabbing start sets the tone for your entire speech and decides if your audience will remain engaged. From anecdotes to powerful quotes, there are myriad ways to hook your listeners from the get-go. We'll explore these techniques and how to choose the right one for your specific audience.

The element of surprise is often an effective tool in capturing attention. When the unexpected happens, people are naturally drawn in. Whether it's a bold statement or a rhetorical question, breaking the norm can be a game-changer. This section elaborates on creative ways to incorporate surprises into your openings while maintaining relevance to your topic.

Furthermore, the first impression also involves your presence and demeanor. Non-verbal communication, such as body language and facial expressions, plays a significant role. We'll discuss how to project confidence and connect with your audience before you even utter a word. Techniques like maintaining eye contact and using purposeful gestures will be dissected in detail.

Storytelling is another powerful method to captivate your audience. Humans are naturally inclined towards stories, and when your speech starts with a compelling narrative, it resonates more deeply. This chapter will cover the art of storytelling, from crafting relatable characters to building tension and delivering a satisfying resolution.

Lastly, understanding your audience is crucial. Tailoring your opening to their interests and expectations ensures you strike a chord from the outset. We'll delve into audience analysis and how to customize your introduction to maximize impact. By the end of this chapter, you'll have a toolkit of strategies to capture and maintain your audience's attention.

2

Chapter 2: Structuring for Impact

A well-structured speech is like a well-built house; it stands strong and serves its purpose effectively. This chapter focuses on organizing your speech in a way that enhances clarity and impact. We'll explore various speech structures and how to choose the one that best suits your message and audience.

The classic three-part structure—introduction, body, and conclusion—forms the backbone of many successful speeches. We'll break down each component, providing tips on how to construct engaging introductions, informative and persuasive bodies, and memorable conclusions. Understanding this framework is essential for any aspiring speaker.

Transitions are the glue that holds your speech together. Smooth and logical transitions between points help maintain flow and keep your audience engaged. This section will cover different types of transitions and how to use them effectively. Whether you're moving from one argument to another or from storytelling to factual information, mastering transitions is key.

Another critical aspect is the use of visual aids. Whether it's slides, charts, or props, visual aids can enhance understanding and retention of your message. We'll discuss how to integrate visual aids seamlessly into your speech and avoid common pitfalls, such as overloading your audience with too much information.

Repetition and emphasis are powerful tools in speechmaking. Reiterating key points ensures they stick with your audience. We'll explore techniques for effective repetition and how to emphasize crucial aspects of your message without sounding redundant. By the end of this chapter, you'll be equipped to structure your speech for maximum impact and coherence.

3

Chapter 3: The Power of Words

Words are the building blocks of your speech, and choosing the right ones can make all the difference. This chapter delves into the art of selecting words that resonate, persuade, and inspire. We'll explore the nuances of language and how to use them to your advantage.

The choice of vocabulary can set the tone of your speech. We'll discuss how to select words that match the formality and mood of your event. Whether you're speaking at a corporate meeting or a casual gathering, your word choice should align with the occasion and audience expectations.

Rhetorical devices are powerful tools in a speaker's arsenal. From metaphors and similes to alliteration and antithesis, we'll cover a range of techniques that can add flair to your speech. This section will provide examples and tips on how to incorporate these devices effectively.

Conciseness and clarity are paramount. We'll explore strategies for eliminating fluff and getting straight to the point. Being concise doesn't mean being brief; it means delivering your message in the most effective way possible. This chapter will teach you how to trim the fat from your speech without losing its essence.

Emotional appeal is another critical aspect. Words have the power to evoke emotions, and a speech that resonates emotionally with the audience is more likely to leave a lasting impact. We'll discuss how to craft emotionally charged sentences and build empathy with your listeners.

Lastly, we'll cover the importance of practicing and refining your word choice. Even the most eloquent speakers go through multiple drafts to perfect their speeches. This chapter will provide tips on how to revise and polish your speech to ensure every word serves its purpose.

4

Chapter 4: Mastering Delivery

A speech is more than just words; it's also about how you deliver them. This chapter focuses on the various elements of speech delivery that can enhance or detract from your message. From tone and pace to body language and eye contact, we'll cover all the bases to help you master your delivery.

The tone of your voice sets the emotional backdrop for your speech. We'll explore how to vary your tone to match the content of your speech and keep your audience engaged. Whether you're delivering a serious message or a lighthearted story, your tone should reflect the mood you want to convey.

Pacing is another critical aspect of delivery. Speaking too fast can overwhelm your audience, while speaking too slowly can bore them. We'll provide tips on how to find the right pace for your speech and use pauses effectively to emphasize key points.

Body language is a powerful form of non-verbal communication. We'll discuss how to use gestures, facial expressions, and posture to reinforce your message. This section will provide practical exercises to help you become more aware of your body language and use it to your advantage.

Eye contact is essential for building a connection with your audience. We'll explore techniques for maintaining eye contact with individuals in the crowd and creating a sense of intimacy even in large venues. This chapter will also cover how to handle nerves and avoid common pitfalls, such as staring at your notes or looking at the floor.

Lastly, we'll discuss the importance of rehearsing your delivery. Practice makes perfect, and this chapter will provide tips on how to rehearse effectively, from recording yourself to seeking feedback from others. By the end of this chapter, you'll be equipped to deliver your speech with confidence and charisma.

5

Chapter 5: Engaging Your Audience

Engagement is the key to a memorable speech. This chapter delves into strategies for keeping your audience actively involved and invested in your message. From interactive techniques to leveraging audience feedback, we'll explore various methods to boost engagement.

Asking questions is a simple yet effective way to engage your audience. Whether rhetorical or direct, questions can stimulate thinking and encourage participation. We'll discuss how to craft impactful questions and integrate them smoothly into your speech.

Interactive activities, such as polls or group discussions, can also enhance engagement. This section will provide ideas for incorporating interactive elements into your speech without disrupting its flow. These activities can make your speech more dynamic and memorable.

Storytelling, as mentioned earlier, is a powerful tool for engagement. We'll delve deeper into how to use stories to connect with your audience emotionally and intellectually. Real-life anecdotes and relatable scenarios can make your message more relatable and impactful.

Humor is another effective engagement tool. When used appropriately, humor can lighten the mood and make your speech more enjoyable. We'll discuss how to incorporate humor without detracting from your message and how to gauge your audience's response.

Finally, we'll cover the importance of listening to your audience. Effective communication is a two-way street, and being attuned to your audience's reactions can help you adjust your delivery in real-time. This chapter will provide tips on how to read your audience's body language and respond to their feedback, ensuring a more interactive and engaging experience.

6

Chapter 6: Crafting a Memorable Conclusion

The conclusion of your speech is your final opportunity to leave a lasting impression. This chapter focuses on crafting powerful endings that resonate with your audience long after your speech is over. We'll explore various techniques for creating memorable conclusions.

Summarizing key points is a common and effective way to conclude a speech. We'll discuss how to concisely recap your main arguments and reinforce your message. This section will provide tips on avoiding redundancy while ensuring your audience walks away with the core takeaways.

A call to action can leave a strong impact. Whether you want your audience to change their behavior, take specific steps, or simply reflect on your message, a clear and compelling call to action can make your conclusion more powerful. We'll explore different types of calls to action and how to craft them effectively.

Quotations and anecdotes are also effective ways to end a speech. A well-chosen quote can encapsulate your message and leave a lasting impression. Similarly, a final story or anecdote can provide a poignant or thought-provoking ending. We'll provide examples and tips for using these techniques.

Creating a sense of closure is essential for a satisfying conclusion. We'll discuss how to tie up loose ends and provide a sense of resolution. This section will cover techniques for bringing your speech full circle, ensuring your ending feels complete and fulfilling.

Lastly, we'll emphasize the importance of rehearsing your conclusion. Practicing your ending ensures you deliver it smoothly and confidently. This chapter will provide tips on how to refine and polish your conclusion to leave your audience breathless and standing in ovation.

7

Chapter 7: The Role of Emotion

Emotion is at the heart of every great speech. This chapter delves into the role of emotion in public speaking and how to harness its power to connect with your audience on a deeper level. We'll explore techniques for evoking emotions and making your speech more impactful.

Understanding the emotional arc of your speech is crucial. Just like a story, a speech should have an emotional journey that takes your audience through various feelings and experiences. We'll discuss how to craft an emotional arc that aligns with your message and keeps your audience engaged.

Empathy is a powerful tool in public speaking. When your audience feels that you understand and share their emotions, they are more likely to be receptive to your message. This section will cover techniques for building empathy, such as sharing personal stories and showing genuine concern for your audience's well-being.

Humor, as mentioned in previous chapters, can also play a significant role in evoking emotions. Laughter can create a sense of connection and make your speech more enjoyable. We'll delve deeper into how to use humor appropriately and effectively without undermining the seriousness of your message.

Pathos, or the appeal to emotion, is one of the three pillars of persuasion alongside ethos (credibility) and logos (logic). We'll explore how to use pathos to persuade your audience and strengthen your arguments. This chapter will provide examples of emotional appeals and how to integrate them seamlessly into your speech.

Lastly, we'll discuss the importance of authenticity in evoking emotions. Audiences can sense when a speaker is being genuine, and authenticity can enhance the emotional impact of your speech. This chapter will provide tips on how to be authentic and emotionally present during your speech, ensuring a deeper connection with your audience.

8

Chapter 8: Overcoming Fear and Anxiety

Public speaking anxiety is a common hurdle for many people. This chapter focuses on strategies for overcoming fear and anxiety, helping you become a more confident and effective speaker. We'll explore various techniques, from mental preparation to physical exercises, that can help you manage your nerves.

Understanding the root causes of your anxiety is the first step toward overcoming it. We'll discuss common sources of public speaking fear, such as fear of judgment or fear of failure, and provide strategies for addressing these concerns. By identifying and understanding your fears, you can begin to take steps to overcome them.

Mental preparation is crucial for managing anxiety. Visualization, positive self-talk, and mindfulness are powerful tools for calming your mind and boosting your confidence. This section will provide practical exercises for mental preparation, helping you enter the speaking arena with a positive mindset.

Physical exercises can also help alleviate anxiety. Deep breathing, progressive muscle relaxation, and stretching can reduce physical tension and promote relaxation. We'll explore these techniques in detail and provide tips on incorporating them into your pre-speech routine.

Practice and familiarity are key to building confidence. The more you practice your speech, the more comfortable you will become with its content and delivery. This chapter will provide tips on how to practice effectively, from rehearsing in front of a mirror to seeking feedback from trusted friends or colleagues.

Lastly, we'll discuss the importance of self-compassion and resilience. Public speaking is a skill that improves with time and experience, and it's important to be kind to yourself as you learn and grow. This chapter will provide encouragement and strategies for building resilience, helping you stay motivated and confident in your public speaking journey.

9

Chapter 9: The Impact of Visual Aids

Visual aids can enhance the effectiveness of your speech by providing additional context and engaging your audience visually. This chapter focuses on the use of visual aids, such as slides, charts, and props, to support and enhance your message.

Choosing the right visual aids is crucial. We'll discuss different types of visual aids and how to select the ones that best complement your speech. Whether you're presenting data, illustrating a concept, or adding a visual element to your story, your visual aids should align with your message and enhance your audience's understanding.

Designing effective slides is an art in itself. We'll explore best practices for slide design, from choosing appropriate fonts and colors to organizing information in a clear and visually appealing manner. This section will provide tips on creating slides that are both informative and engaging.

Integrating visual aids seamlessly into your speech is essential for maintaining flow and coherence. We'll discuss techniques for introducing and referencing visual aids without disrupting your delivery. This chapter will provide examples of how to smoothly incorporate visual aids into different parts of your speech.

Props can also be powerful visual aids. Whether it's a physical object that relates to your message or a demonstration that illustrates a key point, props can add a tactile and interactive element to your speech. We'll explore creative ways to use props effectively and ensure they enhance rather than distract from your message.

Lastly, we'll cover the importance of rehearsing with your visual aids. Practicing with your slides, charts, or props ensures you are comfortable using them and can avoid any technical difficulties. This chapter will provide tips on how to rehearse effectively with your visual aids, ensuring a smooth and polished delivery.

10

Chapter 10: Connecting with Diverse Audiences

In today's globalized world, speakers often find themselves addressing diverse audiences with varying backgrounds, cultures, and perspectives. This chapter focuses on strategies for connecting with diverse audiences and ensuring your message resonates with everyone.

Understanding your audience is the first step toward effective communication. We'll discuss techniques for audience analysis, such as researching demographics, cultural backgrounds, and interests. By gaining a deeper understanding of your audience, you can tailor your message to meet their needs and expectations.

Cultural sensitivity is crucial when addressing diverse audiences. We'll explore the importance of being mindful of cultural differences and avoiding stereotypes or assumptions. This section will provide tips on how to communicate respectfully and inclusively, ensuring your message is well-received by all.

Adapting your language and style to suit different audiences is another key aspect of connecting with diverse groups. We'll discuss how to adjust your tone, vocabulary, and delivery style to match the preferences and expectations of your audience. This chapter will provide examples of how to adapt your speech for different cultural contexts.

Engaging with your audience through interactive techniques can also help bridge cultural gaps. We'll explore methods such as asking questions, encouraging participation, and incorporating audience feedback. By involving your audience in your speech, you can create a more dynamic and inclusive experience.

Lastly, we'll cover the importance of continuous learning and growth. Public speaking is an evolving skill, and staying open to feedback and new experiences can help you become a more effective and adaptable speaker. This chapter will provide tips on how to seek feedback, reflect on your experiences, and continue improving your public speaking skills.

11

Chapter 11: Handling Q&A Sessions

Q&A sessions are an integral part of many public speaking engagements. This chapter focuses on strategies for handling questions and answers effectively, ensuring you remain confident and composed during this interactive segment.

Preparing for potential questions is the first step toward a successful Q&A session. We'll discuss how to anticipate likely questions and prepare thoughtful responses. This section will provide tips on conducting research, understanding your audience's concerns, and crafting clear and concise answers.

Listening actively to the questions is crucial for providing effective responses. We'll explore techniques for active listening, such as maintaining eye contact, nodding, and paraphrasing the question. By demonstrating that you are fully engaged, you can build rapport with your audience and provide more relevant answers.

Managing challenging questions can be daunting, but with the right strategies, you can handle them with grace and confidence. We'll discuss techniques for addressing difficult or confrontational questions, such as staying calm, acknowledging the questioner's perspective, and providing balanced responses.

Structuring your answers is important for clarity and coherence. We'll explore methods for organizing your responses, such as using the "PREP"

(Point, Reason, Example, Point) framework. This chapter will provide examples of how to structure your answers effectively, ensuring your audience understands and appreciates your responses.

Lastly, we'll cover the importance of practicing your Q&A skills. Just like your speech, the Q&A session requires preparation and rehearsal. This chapter will provide tips on how to practice effectively, from conducting mock Q&A sessions to seeking feedback from trusted colleagues or mentors. By the end of this chapter, you'll be equipped to handle any question with confidence and poise.

12

Chapter 12: The Journey of Continuous Improvement

Public speaking is a skill that evolves with practice and experience. This final chapter focuses on the journey of continuous improvement, providing strategies for ongoing learning and growth in your public speaking endeavors.

Seeking feedback is essential for improvement. We'll discuss how to solicit constructive feedback from your audience, peers, and mentors. This section will provide tips on how to receive feedback gracefully and use it to refine your skills.

Reflecting on your experiences is another key aspect of continuous improvement. We'll explore techniques for self-reflection, such as journaling and recording your speeches. By analyzing your performances, you can identify areas for improvement and build on your strengths.

Embracing new opportunities is crucial for growth. We'll discuss the importance of stepping out of your comfort zone and seeking diverse speaking engagements. This chapter will provide tips on how to find new opportunities, from joining public speaking clubs to participating in conferences and workshops.

Staying updated with the latest trends and techniques in public speaking is also important. We'll explore resources for ongoing learning, such as books, podcasts, and online courses. By staying informed, you can continue to evolve and adapt your speaking style to meet changing audience expectations.

Lastly, we'll emphasize the importance of perseverance and resilience. Public speaking is a journey, and setbacks and challenges are part of the process. This chapter will provide encouragement and strategies for staying motivated and committed to your growth. By the end of this chapter, you'll be equipped with a mindset of continuous improvement, ensuring your journey as a public speaker is ever-evolving and fulfilling.

13

Chapter 13: Utilizing Voice Modulation

Voice modulation is an essential skill for any public speaker. This chapter delves into the various aspects of voice modulation and how to use it to enhance your speech. From pitch and volume to pace and pauses, we'll explore the nuances of vocal delivery that can captivate and persuade your audience.

Pitch variation adds dynamism to your speech. We'll discuss how to use high and low pitches to emphasize key points and convey different emotions. This section will provide exercises to help you practice and develop your pitch control.

Volume control is another critical aspect of voice modulation. Speaking too loudly or too softly can affect the clarity and impact of your message. We'll explore techniques for adjusting your volume to suit different parts of your speech and ensure your audience hears you clearly.

Pacing plays a significant role in maintaining audience engagement. We'll discuss how to vary your speaking speed to match the content and mood of your speech. This section will provide tips on how to use pauses effectively to add emphasis and allow your audience to absorb your message.

Intonation and stress are also important elements of voice modulation. We'll explore how to use intonation to convey meaning and emotion, and how to stress key words and phrases to highlight their importance. This chapter will provide practical exercises to help you develop your intonation and stress patterns.

Lastly, we'll discuss the importance of vocal health and maintenance. Taking care of your voice ensures you can deliver your speech effectively and without strain. This section will provide tips on vocal warm-ups, hydration, and other practices to keep your voice in top condition.

14

Chapter 14: The Psychology of Persuasion

Understanding the psychology of persuasion can give you a significant advantage as a public speaker. This chapter delves into the principles of persuasion and how to apply them to craft compelling and influential speeches. We'll explore various psychological techniques that can help you persuade and motivate your audience.

The principle of reciprocity is one of the foundational elements of persuasion. When you give something to your audience, they are more likely to feel obligated to reciprocate. We'll discuss how to use reciprocity in your speech, such as by sharing valuable information or offering assistance, to build goodwill and influence your audience.

Social proof is another powerful persuasion technique. People are more likely to follow the actions of others, especially those they respect or admire. We'll explore how to incorporate social proof into your speech, such as by citing testimonials, case studies, or endorsements from credible sources.

Scarcity creates a sense of urgency and motivates people to take action. When something is perceived as limited or exclusive, it becomes more desirable. We'll discuss how to use scarcity in your speech, such as by highlighting limited-time offers or unique opportunities, to encourage your audience to act.

The principle of authority involves establishing your credibility and expertise. People are more likely to be persuaded by someone they perceive as knowledgeable and trustworthy. We'll explore how to build and convey authority in your speech, such as by sharing your qualifications, experiences, and success stories.

Lastly, we'll cover the importance of consistency and commitment. People are more likely to follow through on actions that align with their values and commitments. We'll discuss how to align your message with your audience's beliefs and encourage them to commit to specific actions. This chapter will provide practical examples and tips for applying these psychological principles to enhance your persuasive abilities.

15

Chapter 15: The Role of Technology in Modern Public Speaking

In the digital age, technology plays a significant role in public speaking. This chapter focuses on how to leverage technology to enhance your speech and reach a broader audience. From online presentations to social media engagement, we'll explore various tools and platforms that can support your public speaking efforts.

Virtual presentations have become increasingly common, especially in a post-pandemic world. We'll discuss best practices for delivering effective virtual speeches, such as using high-quality audio and video equipment, engaging your audience through interactive features, and overcoming common technical challenges.

Presentation software, such as PowerPoint and Prezi, can enhance your speech with visual aids and multimedia elements. We'll explore how to use these tools effectively, from designing visually appealing slides to incorporating videos and animations. This section will provide tips on avoiding common pitfalls, such as overly complex slides or technical glitches.

Social media offers a powerful platform for reaching and engaging with your audience. We'll discuss how to use social media to promote your speeches, share your message, and connect with your audience. This chapter will provide tips on creating engaging content, leveraging hashtags and trends, and building an online presence.

Live streaming is another valuable tool for public speakers. Platforms such as YouTube, Facebook Live, and Zoom allow you to broadcast your speech to a global audience. We'll explore best practices for live streaming, from setting up your equipment to interacting with your online audience in real time.

Lastly, we'll cover the importance of staying updated with technological advancements. The world of technology is constantly evolving, and staying informed about the latest tools and trends can help you remain relevant and effective as a public speaker. This chapter will provide resources for ongoing learning and encourage you to embrace new technologies to enhance your public speaking skills.

By the end of these additional chapters, you'll have a comprehensive understanding of the various aspects of public speaking, from mastering vocal delivery to leveraging technology. Whether you're a seasoned speaker or just starting your journey, "The Blueprint of Standing Ovations: Crafting Speeches That Leave Audiences Breathless" will equip you with the knowledge and tools to captivate and inspire any audience.

Book Description

Do you dream of standing ovations, captivated audiences, and speeches that leave people breathless? "The Blueprint of Standing Ovations" is your ultimate guide to mastering the art of public speaking. This comprehensive book provides you with the tools, techniques, and strategies to craft and deliver powerful speeches that resonate with any audience.

From capturing attention with compelling openings to structuring your speech for maximum impact, this book covers every aspect of public speaking. You'll learn how to choose the right words, master your delivery, engage your audience, and create memorable conclusions. With chapters dedicated to overcoming fear and anxiety, utilizing visual aids, connecting with diverse audiences, and handling Q&A sessions, you'll be well-equipped to handle any speaking engagement with confidence.

The book also explores the psychological principles of persuasion, the role of emotion in public speaking, and the importance of continuous improvement. Whether you're a seasoned speaker looking to refine your skills or a beginner taking your first steps, "The Blueprint of Standing Ovations" offers practical advice, insightful tips, and inspiring examples to help you become a more effective and impactful speaker.

Get ready to captivate, inspire, and leave your audience on their feet with "The Blueprint of Standing Ovations."

www.ingramcontent.com/pod-product-compliance
Lightning Source LLC
LaVergne TN
LVHW020502080526
838202LV00057B/6117